SUGGESTED FURTHER READING

Atkins, C.P. **Canadian Pacific Selkirks;** Profile Publications, Windsor, England, 1973.

Berton, Pierre **The Last Spike;** McClelland and Stewart Limited, Toronto/Montreal, 1971.

Canadian Pacific **Canadian Pacific Facts and Figures;** Canadian Pacific Foundation Library, Montreal, Quebec, 1937.

Dorin, P.C. **Canadian Pacific Railway;** Superior Publishing Company, Seattle, Washington, 1974.

Kaye Lamb, W. **History of the Canadian Pacific Railway;** Macmillan Publishing Co., Inc., New York, New York, 1977.

Lavallée, Omer **Van Horne's Road;** Railfare Enterprises Limited, Montreal, Quebec, 1974.

Legget, R.F. **Canadian Railways in Pictures;** Douglas, David and Charles, Vancouver, B.C., 1977.

Legget, R.F. **Railroads of Canada;** Douglas, David and Charles, Vancouver, B.C., 1973.

Nock, O.S. **Railways of Canada;** Adam and Charles Black, London, England, 1973.

Railfare **Canadian Pacific Railway Annotated Time-table for 1892;** Railfare Enterprises Limited, Montreal, Quebec, Undated.

STATION DISTANCES FROM CALGARY

	Mileage	Elevation (feet)			Mileage	Elevation (feet)			Mileage	Elevation (feet)
Calgary	—	3,438		Lake Louise	116.6	5,050		Glenogle	164.3	2,921
Keith	9.6	3,525		Stephen	122.2	5,332		Golden	171.6	2,583
Kananaskis	54.3	4,100		Hector	125.0	5,213		Rogers	204.4	2,592
Canmore	67.1	4,295	Laggan Subdivision	Partridge	127.8	4,927	Mountain Subdivision	Stoney Creek	214.3	3,565
Anthracite	77.2	4,350		Yoho	129.8	4,725		Glacier	222.1	3,778
Banff	81.9	4,534		Cathedral	132.4	4,502		Illecillewaet	234.9	3,593
Massive	93.0	4,593		Field	136.6	4,072		Albert Canyon	241.4	2,224
Castle Mountain	99.0	4,676		Leanchoil	153.6	3,674		Revelstoke	262.3	1,494

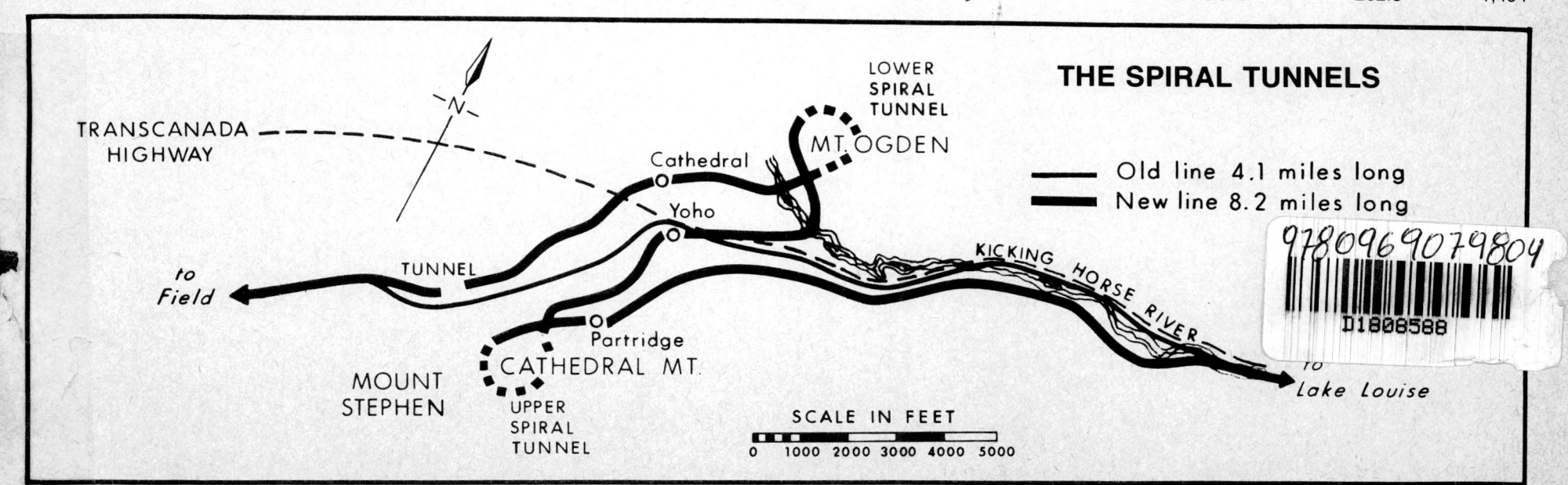

THE SPIRAL TUNNELS

TRANSCANADA HIGHWAY

LOWER SPIRAL TUNNEL

MT. OGDEN

Cathedral

Yoho

—— Old line 4.1 miles long

━━ New line 8.2 miles long

TUNNEL

KICKING HORSE RIVER

to Field

Partridge

MOUNT STEPHEN

CATHEDRAL MT.

UPPER SPIRAL TUNNEL

to Lake Louise

SCALE IN FEET

0   1000 2000 3000 4000 5000

The 1,260 foot difference in elevation between Field and Stephen has always presented problems for the railway. Originally the line was laid with a four mile stretch of constant 4.5% (1 in 22.5) grade. Although this obstacle was successfully operated for 24 years, a solution had to be found and, taking inspiration from the spiral tunnels on the St. Gotthard line in Switzerland, Canadian Pacific engineers constructed a lengthened grade incorporating the two spiral tunnels in 1907-09. This reduced the gradient to a maximum of 2.2% (1 in 45) and, although double and even triple heading was not eliminated, reasonable length trains could be operated without fear of runaways.

Here, the eastbound "Dominion," comprising 12 passenger cars and a caboose is hauled up Field Hill between the two tunnels. The pusher is S2a No. 5811 and the train engine is a P2h No. 5430, a 2-8-2 "Mikado" dating from 1943. Crews did not like the P2's as they were coal-fired (normally referred to as "hay burners") and the wisp of steam on the tender of No. 5430 indicates that the mechanical stoker is in operation. Note the sweat line on the tender of No. 5811. This is caused by the cold water, taken on in Field, chilling the sides of the tender. In the warm tunnels, condensation formed below the water level and this was an accurate indication of the remaining water in the tender. No. 5811 would not need water until she returned to Field.

The caboose at the end of the train indicates that the crew of No. 5430 had been assigned to a freight train and are taking their caboose back to Calgary with them. The green flags on the locomotives on either side of the stack denote that the "Dominion" was running in more than one section. As well as having this visible warning of following sections, whistle signals were, and still are, exchanged with trains standing in sidings. The last section carried no flags and gave no whistle signals.

This photograph showing T1b No. 5920, a 2-10-4 "Selkirk" built by the Montreal Locomotive Works in 1938 being uncoupled from H1e "Royal Hudson" No. 2863 at Glacier, British Columbia, has been extremely difficult to identify. According to CP Rail records, the photograph was taken in 1949 and Nick Morant cannot remember anything special about the occasion. However, the "Royal Hudsons" only worked through the Mountain section on rare occasions, normally when returning from Revelstoke or Vancouver for overhauls at Ogden Shops in Calgary. When this happened, the "Selkirk" was normally coupled next to the train for reasons of efficiency.

It has been suggested that this is the Royal Train which carried H.M. The Queen, though then Princess Elizabeth, on her October 1951 Canadian tour. No. 2863 was the royal engine on this occasion and it did have a special livery, which it would appear to have in this photograph. Furthermore, the train does have an unusual consist and is running as a special as denoted by the white flags beside the stack on each locomotive; so, it is possible that this is the Royal Train and that there is an error in the dates in CP Rail's records. Forty-five "Royal Hudsons" were built between 1937 and 1940. The original 20 locomotives with the 4-6-4 wheel arrangement were built in 1929 and 1930 and were never streamlined. They were known simply as "Hudsons,"

taking their name from that used by the New York Central Railroad for its 4-6-4's.

However, H1d No. 2850 hauled the Royal Train carrying H.M. King George VI and Queen Elizabeth on their westbound journey across Canada in 1939. It was suitably embellished with a special livery and carried a stainless steel jacket around the boiler. Royal crests were fitted on either side of the tender and crowns were attached at the front of each running board. Subsequently, with King George's permission, all streamlined "Hudsons" had similar crowns fitted and became "Royal Hudsons." The right hand crown can just be distinguished on No. 2863 immediately above the cylinder casing.

The train has just climbed from Beavermouth and, in the five mile long Connaught Tunnel, crossed the summit at 3,787 feet. Whereas the Spiral Tunnels lengthened the line and thereby reduced the gradient, the Connaught Tunnel shortened the route and cut back the gradient by crossing the Selkirk Mountains at a much lower altitude. It was constructed between 1913 and 1916, and was named for the Duke of Connaught, Canada's Governor General from 1911 to 1916. The TransCanada Highway now follows a portion of the old railway roadbed which can be seen above the front coaches of the train.

The last of the T1b "Selkirks," No. 5929 hauling a 13 car westbound passenger train past Massive, Alberta in 1950. The frozen Bow River is on the right and the Sawback Range provides a scenic background. The name "Selkirk" was the result of a 1938 employee competition for naming locomotives with a 2-10-4 wheel arrangement and, as the 5900's spent most of their lives in the Selkirks and Rockies, this choice was most appropriate. In the United States, locomotives with the 2-10-4 wheel arrangement were referred to as the "Texas" type after the Texas & Pacific Railroad which introduced this design.

The 5900's were extremely free running locomotives and in dry weather could haul more than 1,000 tons unassisted over the 210 miles of the Laggan and Mountain Subdivisions from Calgary to Beavermouth, British Columbia. On freight service they could take 2,850 tons to Lake Louise unaided but required a pusher for the final 5.6 miles to the summit at Stephen. After the mountain section was converted to diesel-electric operations between 1950 and 1952, the 5900's were all located in Calgary and operated 4,000 to 5,000 ton freight trains over the relatively flat Brooks Subdivision to Medicine Hat (175.8 miles). Occasionally they would work on the Red Deer and Leduc Subdivisions to Edmonton (192.6 miles).

These prairie workings only lasted until the late 1950's. The twenty T1a's were cut up at Ogden Shops, Calgary in 1956 and the ten T1b's were similarly dealt with in 1957. All six T1c's had been withdrawn by October 1959, when they were a mere ten years old.

The second section of Train No. 4 climbing eastward above the 3,255 foot long Upper Spiral Tunnel approaching Partridge siding, 128 miles west of Calgary. The locomotives are T1b No. 5929 and S2a No. 5813. Note the very light smoke from the T1b indicating efficient combustion even though the gradient is 2.2% (1 in 45) at this point. One head-end through baggage car is provided for carrying the luggage of the passengers. Two day coaches are attached behind this and the remainder of the train comprises sleeping cars and a dining car.

From this view, the single stack of the 5900 can just be distinguished. The extended fairing around the stack housed a cowl which was raised by compressed air to deflect the exhaust backwards in tunnels and snow sheds. This was incorporated to prevent damage to the roofs of these structures but, as the deflected exhaust made the cab virtually untenable, the cowls were extremely unpopular with crews and not always used.

The peaks in the distance are part of the Van Horne Range and a shoulder of Mount Burgess can be seen on the right. Mount Stephen (10,495') is on the left and the cover photograph was taken beside the rock face partly hidden by the left-hand signal.

The same motive power combination as in the previous photograph, but with a different train and seen through a telephoto lens. There would appear to be no shortage of steam in the 5900 — the wisp of steam on the 5800 is from the dynamo. At this time, (1946) No. 5813 was still a "hay burner" and was not converted to oil firing until the late 1940's. She was the last of her class to be converted.

The train is about to cross the Kicking Horse River and is heading towards the Upper Spiral Tunnel. It is now extremely difficult to comprehend the barrier that the Kicking Horse Pass presented to travellers in the pre-railway era, but it must be remembered that huge amounts of rock were blasted away to make the original roadbed. A narrow pathway hanging on a cliff was converted into an acceptable, though steep, temporary railway track. Subsequently, the Spiral Tunnels were constructed on a much easier grade and finally the TransCanada Highway completely altered the southern side of the valley.

Built in 1919 and 1920 the 5800's had 58" driving wheels and, with the tender, weighed 546,000 lbs. in working order. Cylinders were 26½" x 32" and boiler pressure was 200 lbs./square inch. Fourteen remained in stock at the beginning of 1950, No. 5814 having been scrapped in 1940, following a mishap.

Train No. 8, the eastbound "Dominion," accelerates away from Banff hauled by an unidentified T1b with Cascade Mountain (9,836') in the background. The TransCanada Highway now cuts through on the right hand side of the photograph but it was a long way in the future when this 1946 shot was taken. Immediately above the locomotive, the old road into Banff can be seen and this still offers the enthusiast an excellent vantage point for train photography.

Current plans call for the TransCanada Highway to be converted into a divided highway at this point. Those who have fumed in the weekend evening traffic jam will welcome this but, before the road can be widened, the railway has to be moved out of the restricted gap in the middle distance. It is rumoured that a tunnel will be cut through the hillside behind the locomotive but the go-ahead for this project has yet to be granted. If it is, Tunnel Mountain will finally get the tunnel it has been waiting for since the path for the railway was originally surveyed.

Until 1923 a coal mine at Bankhead produced subanthracite and the branch line from the mine joined the main line at the foot of Cascade Mountain, one mile west of this point. The right of way can still be observed near the traffic circle outside Banff. Over four million tons of coal were produced from this mine before the seam ran out.

Taken from the old road into Banff shown in the previous photograph and looking towards Anthracite, this view illustrates T1b No. 5927 approaching Banff with the "Dominion" on an extremely cold day in 1950. This locomotive was built in December 1938 and was withdrawn 19 years later.

Ten T1b's and six very similar T1c's were built and could be differentiated from the original T1a's by their semi-streamlined appearance. They had 25'' x 32'' cylinders and 63'' driving wheels. Boiler pressure was 285 lbs./square inch and tractive effort was 76,000 lbs. A booster, which powered the idlers, could be cut in at speeds of up to 12 m.p.h. and this provided a further 12,500 lbs. of tractive effort. Fuel consumption could approach 40 imperial gallons a mile on the steepest gradients. Water consumption between Calgary and Revelstoke was over 90 gallons a mile. The tender carried 4,100 gallons of fuel oil and 12,000 gallons of water. Total weight of engine and tender of the T1b's was 731,000 lbs. The T1c's were 2000 lbs. heavier. Unfortunately, no T1a's nor T1b's have been preserved.

This photograph shows the difference between the telephoto lens used in the previous shot and the normal lens. Both this and previous photograph were taken from the same position, but this one shows T1b No. 5928 approaching Banff with Train No. 3 comprising a box baggage car and 12 passenger cars.

The tower in the middle distance is the balancing tank for the Cascade hydroelectric plant, which is just visible near the tail of the exhaust plume. The Fairholme Range can be seen in the background.

At this point the train is climbing the ruling grade of 1.75% (1 in 57) between Calgary and Lake Louise and, until the early years of this century, trains were pushed from Anthracite to Banff. With the introduction of larger motive power, pushing was rendered unnecessary.

When this early 1950 photograph was taken, Canadian Pacific had 1,718 steam locomotives and 132 diesel-electric locomotives. But the steam era would only last a further ten years and the last steam-hauled Canadian Pacific train ran from Windsor Station, Montreal to St. Lin, Quebec on November 6, 1960. Today, CP Rail has a fleet of over 1,300 diesel-electric locomotives.

The "Mountaineer" bound from Vancouver to Chicago, Illinois at Albert Canyon, British Columbia in 1938. A Class R3c No. 5775, a 2-10-0 "Decapod" acts as a pusher for an unidentified T1a 5900 on the long climb from Revelstoke to Glacier. A stop at the scenic viewpoint will be made three miles ahead so that the passengers can observe the spectacular Albert Canyon and the Selkirks. Note the Mountain Observation Car at the rear of the train. These were referred to as "Hayracks" by train crews and were an excellent means of viewing the scenery. This type of vehicle remained in service until replaced by the current stainless steel Dome Observation Cars in the 1950's. Canadian Pacific was the last major North American railway to use open observation cars, which were confined to the Calgary-Revelstoke section of the transcontinental trip.

They were only used in the summer season and were attached to Train Nos. 3, 7 and 13 westbound, and 4, 8 and 14 eastbound.

The first R3's were built in 1917 in Canadian Pacific's Angus Shops and served as pushers at Golden and Revelstoke for much of their lives. Because they had no idlers, they were very rough riders and unpopular with crews when required to operate at higher speeds.

Canyon Hot Springs Resort is now at this location, approximately 20 miles east of Revelstoke. A few of the buildings still stand, though abandoned, and an excellent campground is available.

S2a No. 5809 acts as a helper for the first of the 20 T1a's No. 5900, as the "Dominion" climbs towards Yoho and the Upper Spiral Tunnel.

The Lower Spiral Tunnel has always been a favourite location for dramatic photographs. With the upper track crossing more than 50 feet above the lower entrance, it is possible to see both ends of a train at the same time. However, the train has to be about 4,000 feet long for this to be achieved and today 80 to 85 freight cars are required. More than 40 passenger cars would be required for the ends to overlap.

Although the Canadian Pacific had some extremely lengthy passenger trains, none was nearly this long and certainly never in the mountains. This 1948 shot was taken by photograph-ing the rear of the train entering the tunnel and then taking another photograph as the locomo-tives passed over the entrance. The two photographs were then merged together to produce this realistic composite. That it is realistic, there is no doubt, for at least two publications have incor-rectly identified it — one claiming that it shows both ends of the "Dominion," while the other states that it shows the front and rear of separate sections of the train.

With today's lengthy freight trains, it is a common sight to see both ends of the train at the same time from the observation point on the TransCanada Highway in Yoho National Park. In fact, some freight trains are too long to see both ends at the same time and the locomotives are approaching the Yoho siding when the caboose enters the lower portal.

An extremely common sight in steam days — the pushers running back to Field for the next series of eastbound trains. S2a No. 5813 together with the P2c No. 5340 and P2e No. 5362 run past Sink Lake, British Columbia, near the west end of Stephen siding. The locomotives have been turned at the Stephen Wye and are coupled together for the 14 mile trip to Field to reduce track occupancy. Pusher locomotives were always turned for the descent to Field as otherwise they were limited to 20 m.p.h.

Temperatures in the cab of a locomotive on the uphill journey frequently reached 130°F and the fireman would replenish the crew's drinking water pail from an ice-cold trackside spring on the Stephen Wye. P2e No. 5361 has been preserved by the Ontario Science Centre, Toronto, Ontario.

Sink Lake is remarkable in that it has no visible outlet. It was probably formed by an ice remnant depressing the soft surface deposits at the end of the last Ice Age. It is probable that water percolates through the glacial debris on the lake floor and resurfaces further down the valley towards Wapta Lake.

With Mount Hector (11,135') forming a scenic backdrop, another unidentified T1b 5900 hauls a westbound 15 car passenger train over the final 1.75% (1 in 57) grade to the summit at Stephen, 122 miles west of Calgary. The Great Divide, separating Alberta and British Columbia, is crossed at 5,332 feet and is the highest point on any Canadian railway. By contrast, the summit in the Selkirks is in the Connaught Tunnel at 3,787 feet, although prior to the tunnel's completion the line reached 4,351 feet in the Rogers Pass.

Unassisted trains of this length were not common in the Rockies and Selkirks and transcontinental trains were frequently divided into two sections for the Calgary-Revelstoke (262 miles) portion of the journey. Although a 5900 had an official unassisted limit of 18 passenger cars over the Stephen summit, it would be sorely pressed to accommodate 15 cars in wintery weather.

The TransCanada Highway now crosses the railway near the last car, and the Stephen siding has subsequently been lengthened at this point. CP Rail has recently filed an application with the Canadian Transport Commission to double the main line between Lake Louise and Stephen. This is necessary to increase the railway's capacity and reduce the gradient on the westbound track. It will cost an estimated $12 million.

Although not really in the Rockies, this photograph of P1n 2-8-2 No. 5258 hauling a mixed train through the Coquihalla Pass on the Kettle Valley Line in 1952 has been included to show the engineering skills of our early railway builders. The line between Hope and Brodie was completed in 1916 across some of the most rugged country in the Coast Range of Southern British Columbia. Snowfall made winter operations extremely difficult and, following serious washouts in November 1959, this line was abandoned. Few traces of the line now remain but the portion between Penticton and Beaverdell is still in existence. Services were discontinued in 1973 and the last train to use the spectacular track was a 4-4-0 dating from the 1880's. This was for filming of the television adaptation of "The National Dream." The trestle bridges in the vicinity of Myra Canyon are especially impressive.

The P1's were light "Mikados," introduced prior to the First World War for freight service but proved to be extremely versatile and could be found on all types of trains. No. 5258 was originally constructed in October 1912 as No. 3912, a Class N3b 2-8-0. It was rebuilt, renumbered and assigned to Class N2b in March 1929. In 1949, it was rebuilt as a 2-8-2 as shown above, and with its tender, weighed 509,000 lbs. in working condition. Boiler pressure was 215 lbs./square inch and the cylinders were 22" x 32". It had 63" driving wheels.

The consist is two box express cars, two baggage-mail cars, two day coaches, a sleeping car and an open-ended cafe parlour car. The two box express cars are carrying overflow express items, and rather than delay the train while they were unloaded, each would be loaded with items for a particular station. They would then be cut out when their destination was reached. Note that they carry the old slogan, "Spans the World."

Looking up the Yoho Valley with a shoulder of Mount Wapta (9,116') on the left and Mount Ogden (8,805') on the right. Class T1b No. 5926 and two unidentified P2's 2-8-2 coal burners climbing eastwards with a 12 car passenger train. The pushers have been coupled next to the train as the engineer of the train engine, No. 5926, has insisted on leading. In this way he would avoid the worst conditions in the two spiral tunnels.

The upper entrance to the Lower Spiral Tunnel is just at the point where the track disappears around the curve behind the train. One thousand men constructed these two tunnels concurrently between 1907 and 1909. Construction was commenced from both ends of each tunnel and the alignments checked to two inches when the breakthroughs were made. The upper tunnel is 3,255 feet long and turns through 288 degrees with a 55 foot difference in elevation between portals. There is a 50 foot change in elevation in the lower tunnel which is 2,922 feet long and curves through 226 degrees.

Takkakaw Falls, the second highest waterfall in North America (1,650'), lie up the Yoho Valley and, after visiting the falls, an excellent view of the Upper Spiral Tunnel can be obtained on the return journey to Field. An interesting sidelight is that the mountain railway scenes for the movie "Doctor Zhivago" were made around the Spiral Tunnels. All trackside markers were removed during filming which was conducted from a flat car propelled ahead of a locomotive.

Castle Mountain (9,030') had just been renamed Mount Eisenhower when this 1947 photograph of the eastbound "Dominion" was taken at mile 97. Note the ten head-end icer cars, which are carrying fruit to prairie markets from British Columbia. Mechanically powered refrigerator cars did not come into widespread use until the 1960's and the old ice house which was used for storing block ice, for cars of the type shown above, can still be seen at Keith, Alberta.

Here, P2h No. 5429 a 2-8-2 "Mikado" of 1943 and a train of standard stock are travelling at approximately 60 m.p.h. on the gently falling (1.0%) grade between Lake Louise and Banff. The P2's had 63" drivers and a boiler pressure of 275 lbs./square inch. Cylinders were 22" x 32" and and the weight of the engine in working order was 339,000 lbs.

P2h No. 5433 is preserved at New Park, Chapleau, Ontario.

As mentioned previously, the name "Selkirk" was adopted for locomotives with a 2-10-4 wheel arrangement. "Santa Fe" was used for 2-10-2's, after the first railway to introduce locomotives of this type. Locomotives with the 2-10-0 arrangement were called "Decapods" for obvious reasons and the name "Mikado" was used for 2-8-2's as the first locomotives of this type were supplied to the Imperial Japanese Railways.

The pronounced cylinder ahead of the stack is an Elesco feed water heater which preheated the boiler feed. They were designed to utilize some of the wasted heat which was exhausted up the stack.

This photograph was not taken in the Rockies, but it has been included to show a mint example of a T1c, the ultimate in steam power built for the Calgary-Revelstoke section of the Canadian Pacific Railway. Elsewhere, it has been claimed that the photograph was taken on the 100 foot turntable at Alyth, Calgary but it was actually taken at Outremont Yard, Montreal soon after No. 5935 had been delivered from Montreal Locomotive Works in March, 1949. The "Selkirk" was undergoing acceptance trials and soon after this, the rods were removed and lashed to the running boards for the deadhead run to Calgary. Because of a lack of oil-fueling facilities, few of the later mountain section locomotives came west under their own power.

Such was the rapid spread of the diesel-electric locomotive that No. 5935 had a working life of only ten years, being withdrawn in March, 1959. In fact, she spent most of her working life on the Brooks Subdivision between Calgary and Medicine Hat. Happily she is preserved and is now in the Canadian Railway Museum at Delson, Quebec. A suitable ending for the last standard gauge steam locomotive built for a Canadian railway.

A second T1c No. 5934 is preserved at Mewata Park, Calgary. This locomotive has been on display since 1960 and is, in fact, No. 5931. It was renumbered as No. 5934 which had originally been sought for preservation, but was already being cut up when the request was received.

Although No. 5935 would appear to have a double exhaust, the rear half of stack housed the cowl for deflecting the blast in tunnels and snow sheds. Note the return to a more normal stack in the T1c's compared with the T1b's which had an extended fairing around both the stack and cowl.

Class R3c No. 5773, a 2-10-0 "Decapod" with a T1a 5900 climbing the lower Kicking Horse Canyon, one mile east of Glenogle, British Columbia. This 1938 photograph shows a passenger train with 12 head-end fruit cars crossing under what is now the TransCanada Highway although a new bridge has since been built at a higher elevation. The 2-10-0 will be detached at Leanchoil and the 5900 will take the train on to Field where another pusher will be coupled on for the ascent of the "Big Hill".

The train engine is No. 5911 (seen in the opposite photograph) and has been identified by the square appearance of the cab. This locomotive was derailed near Illecillewaet, British Columbia and suffered extreme damage during rerailing operations. On being repaired at Ogden Shops in Calgary, it was fitted with a locally constructed non-standard cab. It has been rumoured that the replacement cab came from No. 8000, the experimental high pressure 2-10-4 which was withdrawn in late 1936 and cannibalized to provide standard parts for other 2-10-4's. However, this is not the case. The tender from No. 8000 was retained for further use and was attached to S2a No. 5812.

No. 5773 was built in 1918 and had 58" driving wheels. Boiler pressure was 200 lbs/square inch and the cylinders were 24" x 32". Total weight of the locomotive in working order was 262,000 lbs.

T1a No. 5911 hauls westbound Train No. 3 down the lower Kicking Horse Canyon at Cloister, five miles east of Golden, British Columbia. The square cab of the locomotive can be distinguished in this photograph.

The locomotive is passing under a "telltale," the gibbet-like structure erected to warn brakemen riding on the roofs of freight cars that an obstruction was being approached. Thongs hung down from the horizontal bar and thus provided a physical warning of the approaching danger. It was a hang-over from hand-braking days prior to the introduction of continuous air brakes. Hand brake wheels (known as stem-winders) can be seen on the freight cars in the cover photograph.

The original single-lane Golden to Field Highway can be seen high above the railway. This was an engineering marvel being suspended precariously on the side of the cliff and, in parts, was cantilevered as the cliff face was too steep to allow support from below. Such was the experience of travelling over this road that some motorists had their cars taken back to Golden by train rather than face the return road journey.

Framed by the upper portal of the Lower Spiral Tunnel, SD 40-2's Nos. 5819 and 5674 head a westbound freight train down Field Hill. It is essential to note that both this and the previous photograph were taken by Nick Morant using remote control shutter releases. Venturing into tunnels to take photographs such as this is extremely dangerous and foolhardy.

Cathedral Crags (10,081') stand sentinel over the "Big Hill". The TransCanada Highway, and incidentally the original route of the railway, is the prominent scar above the leading locomotive. The "highline", the track leading from the Upper Spiral Tunnel to Stephen, is faintly visible above the highway.

Both locomotives were built by General Motors Diesel of London, Ontario in 1973 and 1974 respectively at a cost of more than $500,000 each. They are rated at 3,000 horsepower and have a tractive effort of 71,000 pounds. Each unit weighs 393,000 lbs. and has a maximum speed of 65 m.p.h. However, the mountain section of the railway has a maximum speed of 50 m.p.h. for freight trains and there are many local speed restrictions. For example, on Field Hill, freights are limited to 20 m.p.h.

Looking rather like a well-constructed model, the eastbound "Canadian" poses on Stoney Creek Bridge (212.8 miles from Calgary). This location has frequently been used for publicity photographs but, more often, they have been taken from just above rail-level showing the curves on either side of the bridge.

In order to locate the train properly in pre-walkie talkie days, over 4,000 feet of telephone line was needed to communicate between Nick Morant and an assistant at rail-level. Passengers on the train were warned that it would be stopping on the bridge. The track is 270 feet above Stoney Creek.

The original Stoney Creek Bridge was built of wood and was completed in August 1885. It was supported by three piers, the central one being an amazing 228 feet from base to track level. It was replaced by a pair of arches in 1894. This was tested by running six locomotives onto it and it has remained in use until today. However, in 1929, it was considerably strengthened to accommodate heavier trains.

In this photograph, the Dining Car, four Chateau/Manor Sleeping Cars and a Dome Observation Sleeper Lounge Car form the rear portion of the train.

The "Canadian" commenced operations on April 24, 1955 and a new timetable was introduced cutting the Montreal to Vancouver journey time by 16 hours to 71 hours 10 minutes. A total of 173 stainless steel streamlined cars was acquired from the Budd Company to equip the "Canadian" and modernize the "Dominion." Even today these vehicles ride beautifully and are extremely comfortable. In this view, GP-9 No. 8510 and an unidentified FP-7 form an unusual motive power combination heading Train No. 2 down the Bow Valley, three miles east of Lake Louise, Alberta at Mile 113. More normally an FP-7 is the leading locomotive, a situation much preferred by the engine crews. Nick Morant has obtained many excellent photographs on this curve and railway personnel refer to it as "Morant's Corner." This view graced the covers of the December, 1976 "Railroad Magazine" and the July 1977 "Canadian Photography."

Mount Fairvew (9,001') is in the centre of the photograph, and Lake Louise lies in the valley to the right of this. Lake Louise station is located beside the Bow River and between 1912 and 1930 a narrow gauge tramway, using gasoline-engined cars, carried hotel guests to and from Chateau Lake Louise.

The original railway construction camp at Lake Louise was called Holt City. It was subsequently renamed Laggan and then became Lake Louise as its importance as a tourist centre developed. Lake Louise itself, had originally been named Emerald Lake when discovered in 1882 but was renamed in 1884 in honour of Princess Louise, wife of the former Governor General and a daughter of Queen Victoria. The line from Calgary to Field is still referred to as the Laggan Subdivision.

Another modeller's shot, this time to show the construction of a typical snow shed, the lineside equipment and the unlined Mount Stephen Tunnel.

FP-7A No. 1403 approaches mile 134.0, two and a half miles east of Field, with the westbound "Canadian." This handsome 1500 horsepower locomotive was built by General Motors Diesel in 1953 and locomotives of this type have long been the mainstay of passenger motive power. They are referred to by train crews as "covered wagons" but in spite of their age and each having now covered well in excess of five million miles, they still ride smoothly and are capable of high speeds. Since this photograph was taken wider stripes and additional lights have been applied to the leading ends of these locomotives. The lights are set on an angle to provide increased illumination on curves.

The color aspect is a grade signal (as signified by the G) and is the only signal that a train can pass when a stop signal is displayed. They have been erected to provide warning of obstructions on the track and a full freight train can proceed past a red aspect, providing it can be stopped within half the distance that the engineer can see ahead. This system has been instituted to prevent unnecessary stoppages on Field Hill as it could be difficult to restart a full tonnage train.

Taken from almost the same position as the previous photograph, this shot shows SD 40-2 No. 5651 using its 3,000 horsepower to full advantage at the head of eastbound fast freight No. 902. A number of piggyback cars are in the consist. Thirty SD 40-2's (Nos. 5629 — 5658) were supplied by the Electro-Motive Division of General Motors at LaGrange, Illinois, in 1972. General Motors Diesel of London, Ontario, could not accept the order because of prior commitments and the parent company completed the order.

To the left of the track is a snow fence which has been constructed to give warning of an avalanche. When the wires are broken, the grade signals (shown in the previous photograph) are automatically set at stop.

The Van Horne Range is in the background and, to the right of the photograph, the Trans-Canada Highway can just be seen.